BARM
INT
DESI

JOHN AN ERIOR GN

The Monacelli Press
Written with Anthony Iannacci

With many thanks to all our clients, who have inspired us. Also to the many editors who have supported and encouraged our work, to the writers and photographers who have interpreted our projects, and to the many sources, dealers, and collaborators who have helped us to make these homes complete.

CONTENTS

08 INTRODUCTION

10 CLASSIC NEW YORK

26 EXHIBITION SPACE

46 COLOR AND PATTERN

62 TAKING CUES FROM PLACE

72 BLACK AND WHITE

88 LOFTY ELEGANCE

102 RETHINKING THE CLASSIC

112 ACCENTS ON WHITE

136 MAKING IT FUN

148 GEOMETRY PRACTICE

176 INSPIRED BY A COLLECTION

190 RETHINKING THE TRADITIONAL

208 A BARN FOR ART AND GAMES

228 LEARNING FROM ART

246 CREATING A MOOD

264 PHOTOGRAPHY CREDITS

INTRODUCTION

The best contemporary interior design speaks about today: new materials, the latest technology, inventiveness, unexpected use of color, unconventional applications, a piece that looks like it could have come from the Salone Internazionale del Mobile in Milan or Maison&Objet in Paris. Not all of these generally make their way into any single residence, because we seek above all to make our homes truly comfortable, but it's always good to include something "of the moment" to keep a room current. It takes verve, spirit, and enthusiasm on the part of both a designer and a client to use unconventional elements. Hotels and restaurants, which often strive to reflect the latest styles, are frequently the originators of cutting-edge design. Our mobile society is greatly influenced by these trends, and people often request something new they experienced on their travels—scaled correctly—for their residence. These diverse influences appear in the rooms that follow.

Interior design always endeavors to be creative, but the design process is still inevitably and inextricably shaped by convention. It takes knowledge of tradition to distill the canon of historical styles for use in contemporary interiors and to reinterpret their various details in modern ways—and a creative eye to do so successfully. The new millennium is abundant with ideas and opportunities for expressing different genres of design, and any at any given time different styles, different moods, different colors can be appropriate. Now more than ever,

interior designers are expected to be able to switch styles and periods effortlessly, and to be driven by the preferences of an educated client. To do it in good taste is the challenge.

Rooms from the eighteenth and nineteenth centuries particularly continue to inform traditional interiors today, especially in regard to furnishings. Unless a client truly wishes to install a "period" room, traditional conventions are brought into the twenty-first century with an easier and less formal execution, maybe one that is even lighthearted or romantic. Here, layering and embellishing the decorative elements is key—not that every surface or window always needs to be polished, upholstered, or draped. Traditional rooms have specific assignments: foyer/gallery, living room, dining room, library, bedroom, study. Architectural details are applied accordingly to walls, doors, and built-in pieces. The use of color, texture, and pattern may be complex, but can also be extremely simplified, even pared down to one color or pattern. Contemporary art is recommended to tie these spaces firmly to the present.

The terms "modern" and "contemporary" are often used interchangeably although they mean very different things—but they are related. Contemporary just means "produced recently," although in practice it usually refers to an aesthetic of open spaces, a casual atmosphere, and furnishings that are obviously current. Today's modern interior, by contrast, is influenced by elements introduced in the mid-twentieth century, by ideas and concepts that were part of the modernist movement. While forward-thinking for their time, modernist pieces have since become classics, and are ubiquitous. Now, modern interiors can range from exuberant to understated, colorful to neutral to monochromatic, or luxe to rustic. Most modernist furnishings have clean lines; there may be hard corners or soft curves, but all are united by an uncluttered look that is free from unnecessary adornment. Finishes are smooth, whether lacquered or stained. Textiles are innovative but also comfortable or utilitarian. The approach is refined, curated, and thought-out. Modern interior design relies on the details: when so much is unadorned it needs to be executed skillfully.

A relatively new term in interior design is "transitional." This means more than just finding a happy medium between historic and contemporary pieces however. A transitional interior draws on both while striving to be comfortable, soothing, and familiar. Architectural elements may indicate a preference for either traditional or modern, but are counterbalanced by furnishings that stop the architecture from dictating only one mood. Earlier eras of design are drawn upon and reinterpreted with still-recognizable origins under cleaner lines, or, conversely, period details are elaborated on and executed in new materials and finishes. Textiles referencing historic textures and motifs, in particular, are often rendered in new scales or colors. The most overused, abused, and misunderstood term for an interior is certainly "eclectic." Often rooms described as eclectic are little more than a random mixture of styles and objects. When applied conscientiously and effectively however, an eclectic approach melds elements together like varied ingredients in a delicious recipe. Contrasting colors are used to create a dialogue—although often just one color family and one contrast color, to avoid overwhelming the eye. Eclectic interiors need one dominant feature, which should be accentuated by the placement and incorporation of alternative shapes, finishes, and motifs. What unites eclectic interiors and keeps them pleasing to the eye are correlations of one object to another—or the creation of obvious contrasts. Eclectic interiors are popular with collectors; the eye of a collector will have varied interests, but most gravitate to a common underlying concept that appeals to them. Carefully edited eclectic rooms have the potential to be very successful.

Today, interiors are not limited to any one defined genre, so neither are the spaces that follow these pages. Specific furniture, materials, or even architecture does not define a genre or style; it is the overall use of the tools and aesthetic put forward by each that is the defining factor. It is important to have a vision that is focused, but the most important thing is to have imagination.

CLASSIC NEW YORK

Making something classic, timeless, and elegant is a worthy but often-elusive goal for any designer. The ability to even meet it is certainly dependent on the space's location, style, and period. That our notion of what is truly classic is constantly being redefined only adds to the complexity. When John Barman started working on this large prewar New York City apartment, the rooms were already generously scaled, but the spaces were in need of updating. The apartment had been completely renovated; new floors, woodwork, bathrooms, and a kitchen were installed before Barman could choose furniture, carpets, rugs, window treatments, paint colors, or wallpapers. His selections were a highly orchestrated collection of neutrals designed to showcase the client's collection of contemporary art.

The elevator opens onto the apartment's central foyer, which Barman tiled with a highly polished cream-colored stone floor

in a diamond pattern. A lacquered midcentury credenza with brass legs and a pair of glass-and-brass light fixtures fill it with a welcoming sparkle and introduce themes that are carried through the rooms adjacent to this central space.

In the living room Barman established three separate seating areas, the most ample at the center of the room and in line with the fireplace. Two other scaled groupings act as bookends and promote intimate conversation. As with many of Barman's projects, the entire apartment seems designed to foster an expectation of frequent and urbane social engagement.

Right The entry foyer introduces a palette of warm beige and gold that appears throughout the apartment. A vintage 1970s console, purchased in London, sits across from a Sol LeWitt work on paper.

Left and above Reflective surfaces introduced in silver-foil ceilings, silk curtains, vintage Alessandro Albrizzi Lucite candlesticks, a gold-tinted Murano glass chandelier, a highly polished dining set and case pieces, and contemporary free-form wall art all contribute to the dining room's elegant, subtly art deco mood.

Overleaf Bold contemporary art adds dynamism and color to a dining room fitted with elegant traditional furnishings.

Left and above The living room hosts three distinct seating areas: one in the center and two at each end. While the sofas used at either end are identical, the side chairs and tables are not. At one end a T. H. Robsjohn-Gibbings Plume coffee table is used; a French iron-and-stone-topped table rests on the other side.

Previous pages and above Round coffee and side tables of highly polished woods anchor the living room's main seating area. A pair of Jaques Adnet chairs covered in cream-colored leather and featuring thin faux-bamboo legs of brass sit in front of the fireplace. The neutral furnishings allow the art, including an Ed Ruscha, to draw the eye.

Above and opposite The library features wood paneling and a built-in desk, and introduces a palette of muted blues and grays while continuing the blend of contemporary art and vintage accents.

Above Calming monochromatic tones define the master bedroom. Upholstered walls and a matching headboard and curtains help to accentuate a 1940s French desk and chair and a pair of graphic paintings.

EXHIBITION SPACE

Designing and outfitting a home for clients with an impressive collection of contemporary art often means "decoration" takes a backseat, or is confined to refreshing white walls. For John Barman, however, one client's ideas about where certain paintings could hang or sculptures might be installed became the point of departure for intriguing examples of art and design working together.

When Barman started working on this two-story maisonette, part of a larger Peter Marino–designed building but with a private street entrance, architect Edward I. Mills had already helpfully given the original series of cramped, nondescript rooms a dramatic zebrawood entry hall, elegant panels of millwork in the kitchen and master bedroom, and a sinuous new staircase with an art deco–inspired handrail that curved around a freestanding round column.

Barman's work in the living room revolves around a collection of exuberant, stylistically diverse, commanding paintings by Larry Poons, Ethan Cook, Kon Trubkovich, and Jonathan Meese and a massive sculpture by Thomas Houseago. Barman re-created this same diversity of aesthetics in the furniture, including everything from a desk by Jacques Adnet to a nineteenth-century Biedermeier chest, benches from Maison Gerard, a stool by Marc Bankowsky, and a contemporary sofa in gray silk velvet. Indeed, Barman took decorative clues from the art in nearly every room. In the dining room, for example, a painting by Alex Katz prominently occupies the far wall and the furnishings underscore the simple use of color and clean forms that are so much a part of how Katz crafts a portrait. Barman begins with the art to create a lively visual dialogue for each space, ensuring that the exchanges between the fine art and the decorative objects add a level of sophistication and interest to each room.

Left, above, and overleaf A figurative portrait by Alex Katz dominates the dining room and, along with contemporary dining chairs covered in deep orange velvet, infuses the space with a bold sense of color.

Right and above In the kitchen, a long banquette, contemporary art, sleek cabinetry, and a simple-but-unique pattern of floor tiles create a strong sense of rhythm. Classic midcentury furnishings provide the space with an elegant but also utilitarian feel.

Left and above The light-filled living room was designed primarily as a showcase for a collection of paintings and sculptures at different scales.

Left In a reading area at the top of the landing, the furniture is centered in the space to keep the walls available for the display of additional art and sculptures.

Right A bright and sunny paneled bedroom features art of a small, intimate scale.

COLOR
AND PATTERN

John Barman and Kelly Graham share this client's love of strong, bold colors. Although the office had worked together with the same client on other residences, never before had they been quite so adventurous as on this Manhattan penthouse apartment. Situated atop a prewar building, the property was originally constructed as two apartments, one of which was a duplex. The spaces were combined in the late 1970s. At that time, one of the many terraces that wrap around the apartment was enclosed with a glass structure to create a solarium.

The client purchased the apartment for its open views and outdoor space, but the modernist sleek black, gray, and chrome design theme in place at the time did not fit with the age of the building. The client wanted to restore a traditional look that would simultaneously be stylish, upbeat, and very colorful.

The foyer hosted a modernist spiral staircase, which Barman and Graham removed. By enlarging the opening they were able to install a more traditional staircase with a custom railing. A new black-and-white stone floor was laid, and the walls were treated in a lacquered fuchsia with white trim and black doors.

The welcoming new space introduces the dynamic use of color, contrast, and geometry that exists in every room.

A flocked-velvet wallpaper in teal with trim and crown moldings painted to match defines the living and dining rooms. The rugs used here were custom designed in vibrant colors to coordinate with the various and unexpected textiles and art applied to furniture and walls. Just beyond the living room, the den shifts to a green flocked-velvet-on-gold-leaf wallpaper and a custom-colored rug. New wood floors in a herringbone pattern were installed in these rooms and arched openings were built between the foyer, living room, and den/bar.

The long, narrow solarium is anchored by a custom 20-foot-long blue velvet sofa along the window wall and a built-in bookcase on the interior wall. The blue-and-white scheme and the reflective quality of the new flooring make the room appear to float above the city.

Right Arched openings between each room were fitted with substantial moldings to function as definite transitions between spaces focused on strong colors: red, fuchsia, teal, emerald, and blue.

Above Cherry-red lacquered walls and a black-and-white patterned stone floor give visitors to this duplex an enthusiastic reception. A geometric painting by Kelly Stuart Graham hangs in the stairwell. Barman created the interior archways, mirroring their form after the French doors that lead from the apartment's living and dining rooms onto the terrace.

Above, right, and previous pages The coffered dining room ceiling was detailed with an eye-catching pop of teal paint to match the room's wallpaper and trim. Both living and dining areas share the same custom, colored rugs and teal flocked wallpaper. The chandelier is rock crystal and the dining chairs' traditional forms are given an update with metallic pink leather and striped velvet.

Left and above Sitting room walls are covered with rich emerald-green, flocked-velvet, gold-metallic wallpaper. The ceiling features a small cove in gold leaf that reflects the warm light of a vintage fixture into the space. All millwork is lacquered in emerald green and detailed with gold.

Above A bar tucked into a narrow space between the living room and sitting room continues the latter's color scheme.

Right A Fornasetti rug adds a playful note to a guest room furnished with a yellow velvet daybed and Asian decorative objects.

Left and above Soaring glass walls envelop a solarium/library that was formerly a wrap-around terrace. A custom-designed banquette in tufted blue velvet—with built-in blue ginger jar lamps—dominates the long and narrow space while creating an intoxicating place to lounge and take in the view of the rooftops beyond.

Above Blue is paired with shimmering silver in the master bedroom. Custom lambrequins and cornice window treatments and a custom headboard and bed with a quilted base complete the space.

TAKING CUES FROM PLACE

Typically, being inspired by a place means focusing on a quality of light, the specific decorative or architectural history of a building, or the culture of an area. With this Miami Beach project, John Barman and Kelly Graham were driven to create a space that would celebrate the lifestyle offered by its colorful locale: bustling bars, restaurants, and shops. When the pair first saw this light-filled double-height space in a newly constructed beachside tower, it was divided into a series of boxlike rooms. Barman and Graham immediately understood how the space could be reconfigured to take full advantage of its spectacular ocean view and loftlike quality. It could become a vibrant Miami pied-à-terre.

They proceeded to remove all the interior walls. The guest room was reconfigured as a combination office and sleeping area and divided from the living room by a two-story, floor-to-ceiling sliding door, which could be opened to combine the spaces and expand the view for both rooms. Barman and Graham also demolished the original kitchen, knowing that their vision for the space was firmly grounded in the idea of hosting more cocktail parties than Thanksgiving dinners; it was reduced to a bar wall and the refrigerator, dishwasher, and induction cooktop are all now concealed by white custom cabinetry. This bold decision also eliminated the need for a dining table, allowing three cramped spaces to relax into one luxuriously expansive lounge.

To maximize the light, Barman and Graham painted all the walls white and laid white three-foot-square ceramic tile on all the floors—bathrooms and terrace included. Midcentury case goods used throughout the spaces are also white, but bold color makes a strong showing in the apartment in the form of carpets and upholstery with a decidedly 1970s flair. In the living room, a fourteen-foot-long boomerang-shaped sofa is paired with a set of Thonet chairs in fuchsia leather. Colorful contemporary paintings and a dynamic rug inspired by Morris Louis's *Unfurled* series of acrylics command attention in the master bedroom. When all the doors are open, the color functions as guidelines to distinguish where one programmed space ends and another begins.

Right Low bentwood chairs can be easily rearranged around a curved, vivid turquoise sofa and do not impede the soaring view. The canary-yellow sliding door is 18 feet tall and can be used to divide the main living space from the guest room.

Right and above Both the living and guest rooms benefit from plentiful natural light, although cove lighting behind the sofa sets a relaxing mood in the evening. A campaign desk by Milo Baughman occupies a prominent space before the window, and a vibrant painting by Kelly Stuart Graham ties into the space's other colors.

Overleaf Lacquered built-in cabinets conceal kitchen appliances and minimize the presence of the kitchen overall. The white chest is vintage.

Above A sleekly minimalist bathroom keeps the focus on the view while its reflective surfaces keep light moving well into the interior.

Right In the guest bedroom, saturated colors are kept toward the building's core while white accessories and furnishings line the window walls so as not to disrupt the view to the horizon.

Overleaf Art by Morris Louis inspired the master bedroom's custom rug, which is given the counterpoint of a vibrant painting over the room's dresser.

BLACK AND WHITE

This Florida commission gave John Barman and Kelly Graham the opportunity to do something new: to reconfigure, design, and furnish a 6,500-square-foot apartment without using any color whatsoever. The clients, who were moving to South Florida from the north, requested an entirely black-and-white environment.

The apartment's previous owners had combined two units on the same floor and gutted the space, but not anything much more creative than that. Barman and Graham altered one of the original kitchens by enlarging it and reorienting it into a more welcoming configuration. The current master bedroom, which was originally part of one of the living rooms, and the master bathroom were created from the space the second kitchen had occupied. The two original living spaces were consolidated to allow the most spectacular view in the final living room.

In addition to being asked to carve out space to entertain, bedrooms, guest rooms, an office, and a media room, Barman and Graham were given the task of showcasing about 150 artifacts and artworks the clients had collected during their travels to places as disparate as India, France, Turkey, and the American Southwest. To meet this mandate, the designers created an extra-wide hallway and lined it with high-gloss lacquered niches, transforming one of the only spaces in the apartment without a view into a minimalist gallery.

Barman and Graham's primary concern, however, was maximizing the stunning 180-degree views of the Atlantic seen through floor-to-ceiling walls of glass. In fact, the view itself adds the most color to the dwelling. Highly polished white-tile flooring reflects the light coming off the ocean deep into the apartment, providing the entire space with a strong blue-white light. Lacquer, glass, and Lucite pieces continue to reflect the outside light and color in a way that charges the space with brightness. Because the sea and sky are such important elements in this home, the spectrum of their hues seems omnipresent.

Previous pages, above, and right Two identically patterned custom area rugs define seating areas in a loftlike living room. Vintage club chairs with a steel-ring leg detail were covered in black-and-white fabric and edged with black piping to create a sharp contrast with the other off-white seating options.

Left and above The theme of black and white with touches of gold continues into the bar and game areas, which are farthest from the apartment's window wall. Reflective, polished stone floors carry the glow from the ocean and bright Miami sky deep into the space.

Overleaf Graphic geometry continues in the dining room. Here a custom area rug, contemporary mercury-glass chandelier, Lucite candlesticks, and a silver plateau by Charles Hollis Jones make for a visually stimulating space.

Above and opposite Trapezoidal tiles create an op art backsplash in the kitchen while sleek, polished, black granite countertops reflect the light and create a contrast with the white cabinetry. The breakfast table is Eero Saarinen for Knoll and the vintage Lucite barstools are by Charles Hollis Jones.

Left The palette shifts to silver in the master bath. Here a zinc soaking tub and silver-leaf-backed glass wall tile establish the monochromatic, metallic color scheme. The orb-shaped, freestanding towel racks are by Charles Hollis Jones.

Above Double doors between the master bedroom and bath, of black lacquer inset with white geometric detailing, were custom made in Portugal. Similar doors are used throughout the space.

Right Deference is given to stunning views of the Atlantic Ocean in the master bedroom. Here soft textiles including a thick white carpet, a low sculptural settee, and an invitingly furry ottoman add softness while a custom canopy bed in Lucite, chrome-plated steel, and deep black fabric ties into the apartment's overall chiaroscuro theme.

LOFTY ELEGANCE

When a Manhattan loft today reveals any vestige of its gritty history, it's certainly an intentional, sentimental nod to the city's industrial roots. This apartment is polished to such a high sheen that its workaday past is all but obliterated. Barman has created a space that simultaneously maintains a few nostalgic ties to the past while providing for an elegant lifestyle.

For the expanse of high ceilings and windowed walls, white becomes a unifying element and helps to maintain scale. The color also calls to mind the galleries that were, for many, a first experience with loft spaces. Furnishings, objects, and art are artistically arranged here to draw attention to important pieces. Distinct areas for dining, lounging, and entertaining within the large central room also help to give the large space a human dynamic. The only visual partitions enclose a bedroom at one end and a small study at the other. Neutral curtains along the window wall, which extends into both bedroom and study, exaggerate the height and breadth of space while tempering the loft's length by creating visual pauses.

Barman installed dark wood floors to accentuate the volume of the space. These establish a foundation he then continued with dark woods for case pieces and with one large, dark brown custom rug with aqua inserts at various points that suggest spaces for intimate seating arrangements. The rug softens the outsize living room area while also defining the distinct furniture groupings within it.

The kitchen, far from the window wall, is left partially open to the living area; dark woods on cabinets designed to read like warm furnishings provide visual continuity with the rest of the open-plan room. A nearby hallway, otherwise an underused space, was modified and covered in gold wallpaper to host a bar and become an unexpected moment of hospitality and surprise.

Right A painting by Kelly Stuart Graham, a collection of Peking glass vases by Robert Kuo, and dining chairs with French blue fabric backs infuse an otherwise white room with a strong sense of color. The tiered chandelier is Murano glass.

Left and above Chairs, a dining table, and a console united by rich wood tones and high sheen bridge the loft's entry and dining areas and introduce the combination of art deco, modernist, and contemporary details that is present in every part of the residence.

Left and above In the main living space, a large carpet was designed with contrasting blue inserts to help break the open space into more intimate areas. Large windows that run the length of the apartment testify to the building's early-twentieth-century industrial heritage, and are set off by a set of sheer wool crepe curtains that soften the space.

Above and right A Mies van der Rohe Barcelona daybed in midcentury yellow bridges the loft's two main seating areas. One is defined by a sofa and two sets of rounded armchairs, the other by a set of four Milo Baughman chrome-framed lounge chairs placed surrounding a coffee table.

Above Gleaming, dark-stained wood floors unite the loft's public spaces and also lead to the bedroom, which can be rendered private by a set of pocket doors.

Right The long living space is capped at one end by a private study that houses a built-in Murphy bed concealed behind lacquered panels. When its pocket doors are open, it communicates directly with the rest of the open-plan space.

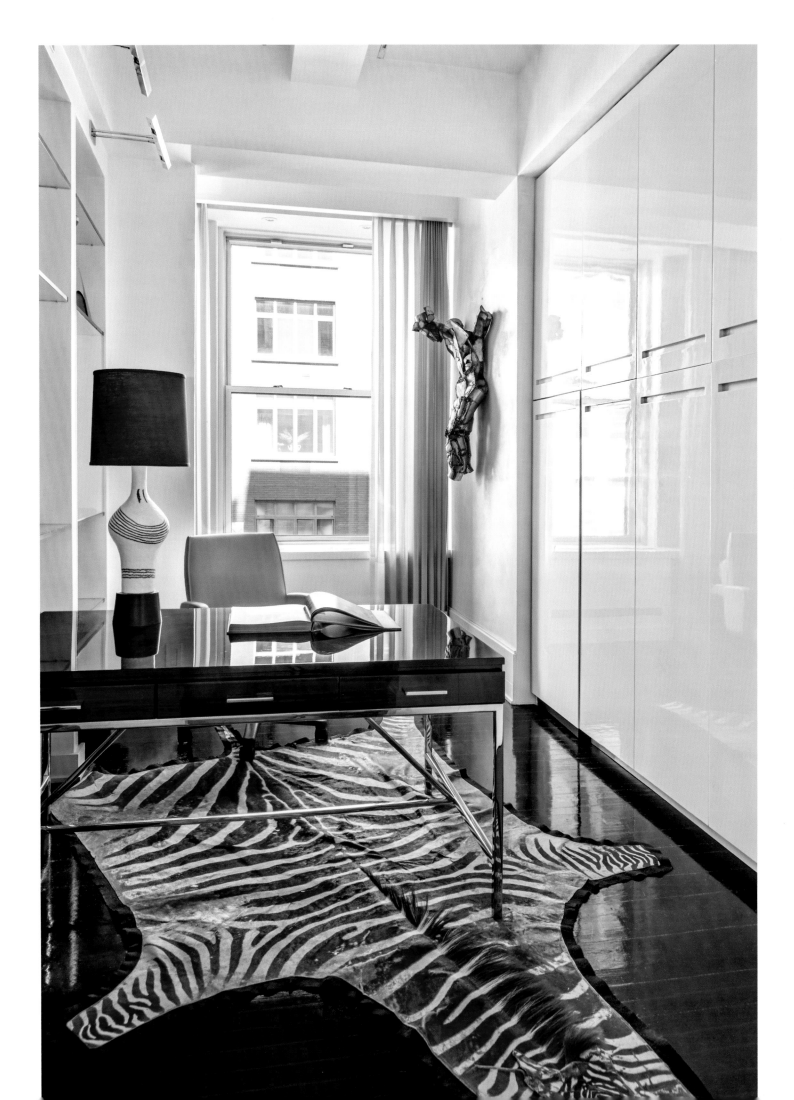

Left and above The kitchen, finished in dramatic wenge wood veneer, is tucked deep into the space's interior and is designed to visually recede from the rest of the home when not in use. An adjacent corridor is covered in reflective mother-of-pearl wallpaper for visual interest, and a bar was installed in the otherwise underused space.

RETHINKING THE CLASSIC

This four-bedroom, 6,000-square-foot apartment in the San Remo, a sought-after 1930s art deco building in Manhattan, seemed like a dream property for clients who love to entertain. However, prewar interiors are not known for being light-filled. Nor did the rooms allow for the free flow between spaces expected in today's more casual environments. John Barman and Kelly Graham knew that this renovation would simultaneously need to celebrate the history of the building and to modernize the quality of the spaces.

To capture as much natural light as possible, they fitted the apartment's small windows with mirrored frames. To increase the home's sociability and render the space more modern, they widened the doorways between public rooms. After that, they let the building's art deco facade provide the reference point for details including lighting, art, mirrors, and the furniture plans as well. Barman and Graham saw the walls as an opportunity to explore both color and materials. The foyer is lacquered in a bold persimmon; the living room walls are covered in a highly reflective gold-leaf paper; and the dining room walls are enlivened by a genteel gold-on-cream pattern of leafy tendrils. Bold geometry that calls to mind the underlying symmetry of the art deco aesthetic and vibrant colors were used on both custom carpets and marble-tiled transitional spaces.

The overall effect remains closely anchored in a notion of classic New York; Barman and Graham's subtle changes rendered these spaces welcoming for a contemporary lifestyle.

Above Art deco detailing on the apartment's crown molding provides the entry, library, living room, and bedroom with a feeling of continuity while underscoring the building's historic pedigree. Symmetry is employed with respect to furnishings and fittings to provide the spaces with an appropriate sense of historic weight, as evidenced in the library.

Opposite In the dining room, a 1950s Italian chandelier is paired with classic Dunbar dining chairs, which were covered in suede. A custom-designed rug features bold patterning as an update to the otherwise traditionally organized and appointed space.

Left and above In the living room, a colorful butterfly painting by Hunt Slonem provided the inspiration for red velvet curtains and gold foil walls. Maison Jansen chairs are paired with three sofas atop a boldly geometric custom carpet.

Overleaf Sand-colored fabric covers the walls and a dramatic headboard in the master bedroom to create a cocooning, monochromatic envelope. Calming blues provide highlights. A custom-designed polka-dot carpet and tiger-print pillows keep the mood lighthearted.

ACCENTS ON WHITE

John Barman purchased a seven-room, early-twentieth-century Hamptons cottage with a 1950s addition many years ago. Since that time the residence has undergone a very carefully orchestrated series of additions and reconfigurations to maintain what originally attracted Barman to the property—a structure that blended beautifully with its pastoral surroundings while fostering a sense of place through charming details like tongue-and-groove walls and Dutch doors.

The entry foyer demarcates the original part of the house from the additions. Barman placed the rooms where an intimate scale would best serve the agenda for the older part of the home—the dining room, library, kitchen, and guest room are all tucked away in its quaint wing. The living room and a second-floor master bedroom suite take advantage of the more ample spaces offered by the newer addition, where the scale jumps dramatically. This shift between rooms was designed to feel very intentional, and celebrates the private and contained rooms as distinct from the entertaining spaces.

The living room, which measures thirty-two by twenty-one feet, hosts two series of elegantly tall French doors on the longer walls. On one side the doors open onto a terrace space that looks over the front garden, and on the other over the patio and back garden. Weather permitting, they can all be opened to create one large indoor-outdoor space that allows for breezy circulation between the front and back gardens. Three distinct seating areas establish intimate spaces within the room, one of which is clustered around a large French stone fireplace and overmantel.

While the charm of vernacular and/or historical details is apparent in every room of the house, the designer has incorporated the most basic of modernism's devices: every room on the interior is painted a stark white. He then went on to challenge that neutrality by incorporating a vivid array of fabrics, objects, and artwork in unexpected combinations of sunflower yellow, bright red, orange, blue, and pink playing off dark wood floors and zebra rugs.

Right A vibrant Dutch door leads to a white entryway full of colorful art and accessories, including a Regency console hosting a pair of vintage concrete seahorses and a Hunt Slonem painting of sunflowers and butterflies.

Above An all-white kitchen retains a country mood thanks to rustic hardware, vintage pottery, and a teak table. Black bamboo chairs add an element of surprise.

Above and right A Moroccan chandelier finished in red automotive paint injects instant festivity into a high-ceilinged dining room that holds an oversized round dining table. Vintage bamboo chairs lacquered black are ready to seat ten. Geometric paintings by Kelly Stuart Graham hang below matching vintage sconces on opposite walls.

Above The study concentrates on orange and turquoise accents. The ottomans are Paul McCobb and the desk is 1940s French.

Opposite The living room, set in the heart of the house, is an eclectic mix of traditional, modern, contemporary, and ethnic pieces. Bold paintings by Kelly Stuart Graham are installed at each end of the long room. A nineteenth-century English wingback chair with accompanying pull-out footrest—both upholstered in red leather—creates a focal point.

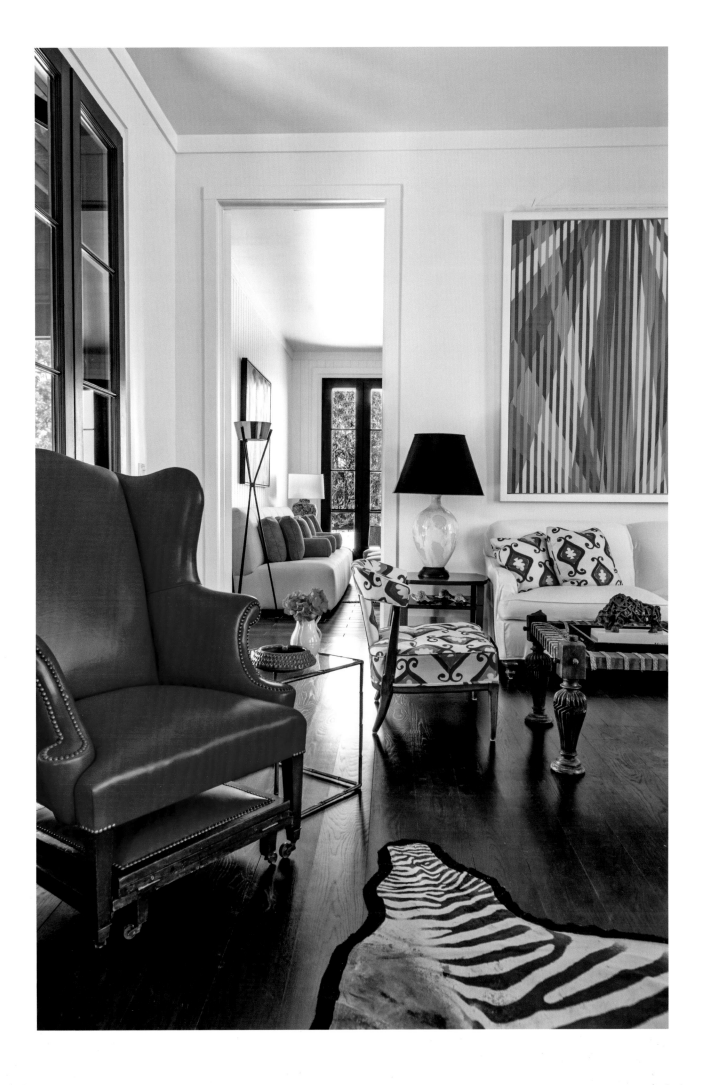

Above and opposite Corals and seashells, along with pottery in cobalt blue, set a summertime tone for the library. An eighteenth-century limestone mantel adds a historical note.

Above Tall double doors lead to the living room and den, while a Mediterranean-inspired stair rail leads to the second-floor master suite.

Opposite A Moroccan lantern illuminates the stairwell adjacent to the master suite, and floats there like a sculptural pendulum. The chest inside the room is mahogany and dates to the nineteenth century.

Left and above Vaulted ceilings allow a custom four-poster bed to fit snugly beneath in the master suite. A painting by Kelly Stuart Graham hangs above a sofa at one end. At the desk by a broad bank of windows, a chair playfully covered in a tiger pattern continues the animal-print theme introduced by the zebra rugs.

Above A small sitting room between the master bedroom and dressing room offers views over the stairwell and out to the house's rear garden.

Opposite An ornate Moroccan lantern and an antique Persian rug bring an exotic note to the traditionally appointed master bath.

Left Pattern appears on a guest bedroom's antique Persian rug, bed upholstery, and the herringbone interior of an eighteenth-century French limestone mantel.

Above An alcove between the kitchen and dining room is enlivened with a simple bar. A pair of cast-plaster sconces in the shape of seahorses pays homage to the seaside location.

Above A row of tall French doors leads out to a terrace furnished with three distinct seating areas.

MAKING
IT FUN

Rooms with strong identities make for the most memorable spaces. The owner of this South Florida house had the courage to incorporate a bold palette of bright turquoise, hot pink, lemon yellow, and lime green, indicating a real commitment to creating a happy, upbeat, and sunny residence that reflects the vibrancy of its tropical surroundings.

When John Barman and Kelly Graham first saw this house, it was dark, drab, and the ground floor was divided into a labyrinth of small spaces. They took advantage of the exquisite waterfront site by bringing as much of the vibrant outdoors inside as possible. The design team proceeded with a top-to-bottom renovation that left only the windows, main stairway, and ground-floor library and guest room intact. With the first floor refashioned into one sprawling space, the high ceilings allowed the light and the view of a lake to become part of the décor. A modernized space was also better suited to the family's casual lifestyle. Since the client loves to cook, the kitchen was

opened to the living spaces so that time spent over the stove could still be time spent interacting with family and guests.

Barman and Graham decided to use an all-white background in the house, and installed a completely white kitchen as well. Saturated colors so beloved by the client were reserved for the home's eclectic furnishings. The design team also took cues from her extensive art collection for the fabrics, objects, and rugs, which stand out, happy and bright, against the neutral background. This strategy also helped to create interest within the home while at the same time focusing attention on the equally lush and colorful landscaping and view beyond.

This vacation residence succeeds at using sophisticated details, but without taking them too seriously. Intense colors along with an eclectic collection of new and custom furnishings, paired with unique and vintage pieces from the 1940s through the 1960s, combines graciousness with a seriously playful ambience.

Previous pages and above Bright oriental prints, Chippendale-style furniture, chinioserie details, and bold contemporary art infuse every room in this house with a sense of whimsy and fun. The colors and shapes of the furnishings evoke the verdant garden beyond. In the dining room, bold floral prints on the chairs are paired with a vintage midcentury table base.

Opposite In the breakfast room, scalloped-back chairs with sea-blue upholstery refer to the seaside tropical setting in both color and form.

Previous pages and above The open kitchen is the heart of the family room. Polished-
brass hardware and blue-green granite counters provide a touch of the nautical.

Above Art by Peter Dayton sets the chromatic mood for a small study dressed in shades of white, orange, and red. Plantation shutters in an unexpected deep orange provide privacy and can be used to darken the room for watching films.

Above The chinioserie theme continues in the master bedroom, where the palette relies on blue and white. A pair of 1970s vintage lamps with ceramic blossom details and a Chinese garden stool bring the garden beyond indoors.

GEOMETRY PRACTICE

Geometric patterning abounds in the full-floor apartment John Barman and Kelly Graham designed to take advantage of 360-degree views of Manhattan. The building, a 1980s high-rise designed by James Polshek and erected thanks to the developer's ability to obtain the air rights above a 1959 landmark Skidmore, Owings & Merrill modernist office building, reveals postmodern ideas about the manipulation of space. The designers decided to embrace them rather than fight them, and developed a series of eclectic spaces, each with its own strong personality that, when experienced together, create a bold and memorable whole.

The apartment's theme is set by the twenty-four-inch square, diagonally laid, black-and-white floor tiles first encountered in the entry hall. This highly polished, oversize stone checkerboard pattern introduces the vocabulary of bold geometry present throughout the apartment. Used exclusively in public spaces, the tile also becomes a wayfinding device, drawing visitors to the areas of the apartment meant for hospitality.

The entry leads directly onto the dining room, which occupies a square corner of the apartment. To foil the room's boxy dimensions, an oversize round table sits on a round carpet insert and one large circular coffer in the ceiling is painted in high-gloss yellow to bring the eye up and to give the illusion that it is higher than it is. The yellow was chosen for its mood-lifting qualities, and because in the evenings, when illuminated by lights recessed in the circle's rim, it gives a warm glow to the room equivalent to hundreds of candles.

Barman and Graham installed a lacquered, cobalt-blue study as a transition between the dining room and the gallery. The vibrant color on the walls and bookshelves—along with a wool carpet and flannel sofa in an identical hue—sets it off from the white rooms that surround it while bringing attention to the books and objects.

The black-and-white floors continue into a bar/lounge room and then lead visitors to an expansive living room. A sinuous, highly reflective chrome room divider with a pattern of convex spherical forms announces the presence of bold geometry here as well. Lacquered walls in a neutral gray bounce light around the space and function as a deferential backdrop to a collection of contemporary and midcentury furnishings and art that fill the broad and unique space.

Left A banquette adorned with pillows and shades in a modern Greek key motif provides a perch in the corner of the dining room for taking in the city view.

Above To give a square dining room dimension, a circular tray ceiling was created and lacquered in a deep yellow, a circular rug was inset into the black-and-white stone tile floor, and an outsize round dining table with a brushed stainless steel top was installed below a midcentury chandelier by Claude Ferre that was originally designed for a casino in Royan, France. The sideboard is by Tommi Parzinger and the painting is by Kelly Stuart Graham.

Above A colorful painting by Agathe de Bailliencourt commands attention below the yellow tray ceiling. The dining chairs, by Edward Wormley for Dunbar, are of ebonized mahogany and rosewood.

Above A painting by Barnaby Furnas hangs in the entry, leading the way into the dining room and introducing some of the colors that are used there. The yellow tray ceiling in the dining room seems to continue the highly reflective theme introduced by the polished black-and-white floor, which ultimately transitions to a circular carpet for the space. The sconce is a midcentury find and part of a set used throughout the entryway/gallery.

Left Bright cobalt-blue lacquer draws visitors from the dining room into the adjacent library. The carpet, a slightly darker shade of the same hue, continues the monochromatic theme of the room and helps the vibrant color feel restful to the eye.

Above In the library, a nineteenth-century Empire console, vintage midcentury swivel chair upholstered in lamb, and contemporary art all come together to create a unique space.

Left and above Stainless-steel cabinets were installed in the bar room, which was created just off the apartment's central corridor. The ceiling is papered in black and silver in a nod to the bold black-and-white stone flooring that flows into the space.

Previous pages and above The long living room is a composition of three distinct seating arrangements and a desk area. One sofa is installed before a mirrored screen of convex spheres, which repeats the theme of the circles within squares begun in the dining room.

Above An L-shaped sofa occupies the far corner of the gray-lacquered living room, along with a vibrant painting by Karin Davie that adds curve. The chrome-plated table lamp dates to the 1970s and is by Curtis Jere.

Above A French desk from the 1940s in sycamore veneer is combined with a pair of Dunbar chairs with Lucite legs.

Right A painting with a nostalgic twist by Paco Pomet hangs above a vintage bar cabinet. A collection of red and yellow vintage glass fills an adjacent niche.

Left Flooring transitions from black and white stone to red carpet to indicate a shift from public to private spaces.

Above A series of paintings by Jeff Lewis greets visitors entering the media room, which offers a vintage Knoll white leather bench as one seating option.

Above A plump L-shaped sofa fills a corner of the media room and is accompanied by a dining table that was altered to a height between coffee table and dining table—all the better to allow for casual dining or working in the cozy setting.

Opposite and above The master bedroom features dramatic black walls, a red carpet, and white accent walls and niches. One corner hosts a wooden desk and vintage Lucite chair. The painting above the bed is by Kelly Stuart Graham.

Above The red carpet continues into the hallway and dressing area. The large scale of the black-and-white stone flooring in the public areas shifts to a smaller-scaled shadow box mosaic stone floor in the master bath.

Right A vintage cabinet in red, white, and black laminate featuring iron legs perpetuates the bath's strong geometry. The painting is by Kelly Stuart Graham.

INSPIRED BY
A COLLECTION

This once-regal Upper East Side townhouse dating to 1870 had become nearly derelict by the time its current owners purchased it, and required an extensive renovation that was a true collaboration between the clients, John Barman, and the architects—the Brooklyn-based DiDonno Associates—to be made an elegant and comfortable single-family home again. The resulting interior showcases the clients' extensive collection of French moderne furniture and decorative objects, and also takes inspiration from that collection in every detail.

Adding a sense of transparency and translucency to this historic structure became a primary concern. In order to achieve this, steel-framed glass doors and walls were used to divide interior rooms and hallways. Similar doors were installed leading to the rear yard. Steel-framed windows also open up views throughout the house. Much of the original detail had already been removed, so Barman and the architect were free to infuse new additions with the seductive formalism and rich textures of the 1930s and 1940s.

The clients had been avidly collecting French art deco furnishings for over a decade when they took on the townhouse renovation, so they had become very knowledgeable about the period.

They understood the value of their collection but were also not afraid to integrate reproductions and contemporary pieces in an effort to create a space that would maintain a polished aesthetic while remaining highly functional. Many pieces, therefore, were custom-made, including an Émile-Jacques Ruhlmann–inspired iron stair rail that winds up four floors, and the master bedroom's red-leather-and-sycamore side tables in the style of French cabinetmaker André Arbus. Decorative motifs were also adapted from rich historical references. The whimsical faux boiseries in the guest room, for example, were inspired by Christian Bérard's painted interiors for the Institut Guerlain in 1939. Portoro marble was installed in the bar area off the hallway and used on a pair of consoles in the dining room that match the living room's high-contrast mantelpiece, adding another reflective dimension that complements the highly lacquered furniture.

Barman suggested introducing contemporary art to serve as a foil to the period furnishings and to keep the interiors feeling fresh. The designer also chose a palette that allowed the best pieces to stand out—taupe, pale smoky tones and olives for the living room and study, lush red for the draperies that light up the master bedroom.

Left The art deco–inspired interior is a composition in muted tones. Charcoal-colored velvet curtains emphasize the height of the room and create a sense of drama as they frame iron casement windows that were carefully designed to contribute to the sense of history that is evident throughout the home.

Left and above Interior room dividers and doors are modeled on the iron windows to provide visual continuity. These paned doors open onto the living room and library. The piano in the living room features an art deco form. The scalloped-edge coffee table made of a boldly striated wood in the library is custom made.

Above and opposite Warm wood shelves make the library an inviting part of the house. A collection of white pottery with a period-appropriate form stands out in striking contrast to the dark wood bookcase.

Overleaf The dining room hosts an art deco–style table with a parchment top. Dining chairs, artwork, and lighting are all drawn from the art deco period and all contribute to a unified vision of subdued elegance.

Left A Jacques Adnet bed wrapped in cobalt-blue leather is fitted with a linen-covered mattress and two bolsters; it is set off simply by a lamp and chair in similar tones.

Above In one of the guest rooms, a Christian Bérard–inspired trompe-l'oeil paint detail on the walls makes for a truly unique, yet simple, space.

Above and opposite Dynamic red is combined with blond woods to create a unique color scheme for the master bedroom. Rich velvet curtains and a custom-finished nightstand with matching red leather drawers are the most dramatic use of color in the room.

RETHINKING
THE TRADITIONAL

Large rooms, high ceilings, and the traditional Shingle Style of the exterior attracted John Barman and Kelly Graham's clients to this recently constructed Hamptons summer home. The interior, however, had awkward room proportions, a lack of architectural detail, and bland blond-wood floors. These were the first elements they asked the designers to correct.

The interiors were essentially arranged as an open, contemporary plan that mimicked some semblance of a traditional organization. Barman and Graham focused on distinguishing one room from another, a challenging task since the passageways between the major rooms—entry, living, dining, and family—were extremely wide. By narrowing these transitions, the designers were able to provide each with an individual scale that would frame the chosen furnishings while also creating more wall space.

They then turned to infusing each newly defined area with a fresh-yet-traditional ambience. Instead of taking their lead from the traditional exterior architecture, which may have called for rustic furnishings consistent with the area's agrarian past, Barman and Graham found inspiration in the elegant country homes portrayed in the grand films of the 1940s and 1950s, such as *The Philadelphia Story*. This correspondence is clear from the living room's furniture plan, where several distinct seating areas—particularly useful in breaking up a large space—are arranged to host large, small, or even multiple groups.

Throughout all the rooms, vintage 1940s, '50s, and '60s pieces are mixed with custom furnishings and contemporary art. Specific colors—such as golden yellows in the living room, oranges in the family room, and greens in the master bedroom—further the design team's goal of bestowing each room with its own personality while also providing a sense of endless summer.

Right A round 1940s hall table sits on a custom-designed round rug in the front entry foyer. Custom paneled millwork was introduced and painted white while the front door was painted black to make it stand out from all other doors in the house.

Left and above The sunken living room hosts three distinct seating areas; two flank the entrance to the room and one is centered on a far wall. Each of the corner arrangements hosts a custom-made corner sectional, and one is accompanied by a pair of T. H. Robsjohn-Gibbings chairs upholstered in a custom honey-toned fabric.

Above The living room is a study in golden yellow. A custom wool area rug in a warm hue helps to ground the large space's various seating arrangements. Vintage lamps and end tables and custom-colored, printed fabrics, along with woven linen textiles on chairs and pillows, all contribute to the soothingly saturated look. The coffee table is finished in a custom bamboo veneer.

Above and opposite The golden hue continues in the dining room, where a straw-colored grass cloth covers the walls. Dining chairs are fitted with raffia backs and vibrantly patterned cushions; these coordinate with the vintage table and other vintage case pieces in the room. Pottery is used here, as throughout the house, as both lamps and accent pieces.

Left An all-white country kitchen is given doses of color with collections of vintage pottery in bold reds, yellows, and oranges. A breakfast nook features a brushed-chrome drum table fitted with a wooden top and chairs made of wood and leather; these add a touch of unexpected modernity to the beadboard-clad room.

Above A series of square lanterns-within-lanterns hangs in the hallway. Dark-stained wood floors run throughout, visually connecting rooms with different functions.

Previous pages In the den, the color palette stays within the realm of sun tones, but moves toward orange. A Werner Platner wire game table and Milo Baughman chairs fill one corner. The round rug, in blocks of yellow and red-orange, was custom designed.

Above The master bedroom continues the color scheme but adapts the sun-tone decorative palette in soothing gold, adding green and blue accents. Vintage ceramic lamps, a striped rug, and patterned fabrics on the seating give the space a fresh, summertime quality.

A BARN FOR ART AND GAMES

Clients who own multiple properties often decide to experiment with one, breaking out of their usual ideas about style to arrive at something whimsical and extraordinary. When a couple for whom John Barman had already designed an apartment in the city approached him to furnish their newly acquired country residence, Barman and codesigner Kelly Graham knew that incorporating some of their clients' extensive collection of contemporary art would be an invigorating challenge—not least because the property happened to be a 10,000-square-foot, nineteenth-century farmhouse and barn that had been united in the twentieth century. Working together, the team turned it into the vibrant, eclectic, and welcoming home they envisioned.

Barman and Graham's clients may not have known exactly what they were looking for at the outset, though they were certain they wanted none of the expected rustic furniture or folk art the historic property's stone fireplaces, wide-plank wood flooring, and rough-hewn beams might suggest. The client's vision for the property was to create a home that would at once celebrate the surroundings and feel playful.

Abandoning the expected, Barman and Graham chose a strategy based on contrast instead of conformity. The designers' choice of bright yellows and oranges—often applied in strong, modern patterns—with a midcentury, California-modern vibe actually serves to underscore the property's antique elements while creating novel and felicitous relationships within the historic spaces.

Barman and Graham started by leaving all the windows bare, even in the master bedroom, in order to allow the light to push back against the weight of the heavy wood and to allow appreciation of the beautiful views. In every room brightly colored rugs with a hip, casual-vintage feel are used as defining elements. In the living room, for example, a large white rug is dotted with green, orange, and yellow ovals that coordinate with a collection of vintage furnishings and objects. To encourage relaxation, Barman added unexpected twists to gaming opportunities, such as lining a custom pool table with yellow felt and endowing the library with foosball and ping-pong tables.

Above and right The rustic building's walls were painted a warm white to both accentuate the art collection and the structure's original beams, columns, and rafters. A custom pool table topped with gold felt occupies a prominent space adjacent to the main living room.

Overleaf In the main living room, a custom carpet with a midcentury-inspired color scheme of red, orange, yellow, and green forms reminiscent of martini olives hosts seating enough for a crowd. Vintage ceramic lamps, a pair of French pendant lamps finished in an original and intriguingly rusted orange, and Hans Wegner Papa Bear chairs complete the dynamic space.

Above and right The media room features an orange sectional topped by an abundance of striped pillows and two round Mushroom chairs by Pierre Paulin. The red ottomans are by Enrico Baleri and Denis Santachiara.

Above A vintage game table and chairs sit in a sunny corner of the living room; their orange cushions play off a lively painting by Roger Brown.

Right In the dining area, leather-strap chairs are paired with a wood slab dining table with natural edges.

Above Contemporary glass vases by Robert Kuo fit well with the midcentury colors and forms used elsewhere in the converted barn.

Right A dining table made from a mill gear, orange-upholstered dining chairs, a custom-designed and color-blocked area rug, and vintage ceramic chandelier infuse the already sunny space with plenty of verve.

Above The game room, in a newer part of the home, features white beams as well as white walls and a sleeping loft. A custom-colored round area rug and vintage chairs covered in wool melton create an island of energetic color.

Left A rough stone chimney edges the master suite's sitting room, which is lined with bookshelves and furnished with comfortable reading chairs, notably one by Paul McCobb.

Above The office holds a desk and chair originally from the United Nations headquarters, along with a tiled coffee table and curved sofa, all atop a bright, rust-colored area rug.

Left and above The master bedroom and bath occupy a lofty space under the barn's gabled roof. The bed's headboard is made from a single rustic wood slab. A custom area rug, vintage standing mirror, chaise longue by Christian Liaigre, and twig chandelier complete the space.

LEARNING
FROM ART

After living in this prewar New York City building for many years the owner acquired the apartment below as well, thus doubling the square footage of this seven-room residence. Architect Alexander Gorlin, who has a reputation for deftly reorganizing historic interiors to meet the needs of today's users, was hired to transform the labyrinth of boxy rooms into a smoothly functioning family home. The centerpiece of the intervention is the light-filled open area hosting the entry, dining, living, library, and music spaces. Gorlin also established a kitchen and office at the back of this floor and a study off the living area. By opening the space from front to back, he was able to let light into the previously double-stacked rooms at the center of the floor plate.

A spiral oak-and-glass staircase with the surprising detail of a cobalt lacquer underside functions as a fulcrum between the public spaces on the lower level and the private spaces above. On the upper level, the architect worked at a more intimate scale. Here a family room is open to the staircase and serves as a transition to the bedrooms beyond.

Barman worked to establish intimate and distinct areas within the open-plan space of the newly created living and dining area. The biggest influence on the interior planning for this duplex,

however, was the client's extensive collection of contemporary figurative paintings. Barman took his cues from the bold stylistic and chromatic variations represented in this exciting and eclectic array.

In the dining room, for example, the acid-green velvet used to cover the chairs and the cobalt blue in the carpet seem to have been directly extracted from the painting hanging on one wall. Continuing the theme of unexpected juxtapositions, in the living room chairs upholstered in ruby mohair and acid-green velvet happily coexist with boldly graphic checkerboard sofas in brown and beige.

Barman is a master at creating separate functions within one wide area and understands that an absence of fixed boundaries allows a space's overall design to resonate from every angle. Here he was clearly inspired by his client's adventurous collection and translated that sense of excitement and variation into the décor.

Right An art deco table sits neatly within the curve of a custom-designed spiral stair of oak and glass. The stair's sinuous underside is lacquered in a dark cobalt blue, a color picked up again as an accent on the runner.

Above A custom limestone mantel relates to the loft's exuberant mood; a cobalt blue Fontana Arte mirror hangs above. Islands of contrasting color inserts in the carpet demarcate distinct seating areas within the space. Vibrant colors and patterns on the furnishings seem drawn directly from the owner's collection of figurative paintings.

Previous pages A library space inset into the larger living area keeps view corridors open to the rest of the room—and the room's art—through wide spaces between its equally wide columns, which also support low shelving units and provide additional display surfaces for smaller works of art.

Left Seating in vibrant gem tones surrounds a piano that occupies the far side of the living room. The study can be seen in the distance. The red carpet to the left shows the location of a reading area.

Above Striped velvet armchairs with matching ottomans enliven a study otherwise devoted to navy blues.

Right and above An art deco dining table and credenza are the foundations of the dining area. The rug was custom designed to reflect the colors in some of the nearby paintings, and the Jules Leleu dining chairs were upholstered in acid green mohair for similar reasons.

Above In this duplex TV viewing takes place at the top of the stair landing, in a space given over to light woods and cheerful pinks.

Overleaf In the master bedroom, relaxing violet reigns. The owner's collection of figurative paintings extends to this room, which also functions as a library.

CREATING
A MOOD

It is difficult to imagine that a 12,000-square-foot exquisitely constructed Shingle-Style home steps from the ocean would require anything beyond the usual beige summerhouse standards to foster relaxation and a sense of removal from the chaos of the city. John Barman's clients had different ideas about what their family's beachside home could accomplish, however. Not only did they encourage him to infuse the spaces with rich, bold color, they also requested he use a painting they had commissioned, depicting a group of Chinese women in traditional dress and seated at a long yellow table, as his point of departure for the interior spaces.

Barman took the challenge and ran with it. His first inspiration was the Royal Pavilion in Brighton, England, a seaside retreat constructed in three stages beginning in 1787 for George, Prince of Wales, who became the prince regent in 1811. John Nash's Indo-Saracenic pavilion is a masterful example of escapist seaside architecture.

This pleasure palace became Barman's muse. The interiors needed to encourage a sense of fun and adventure, but the mandate was to steer away from beachy kitsch. In order to accomplish this, Barman painted the majority of the walls white and let the furnishings, fabrics, art, and objects direct a whimsical-yet-elegant decorative voyage to the Far East.

The foyer serves as an introduction to this exotic world. An oversize pagoda-shaped chandelier is the first of many juxtapositions between the traditional lofty, vaulted space with a grand double staircase, traditional dark-wood floors, white wood paneling, and Asian details. Several Chinese ancestral portraits hang on the upper walls while sinuous Chinese dragons dance around a custom circular rug and down a matching set of stair runners. Mandarin guards flank the entrance to the dining room, which is lined in a bright blue, chinoiserie-style, linen-and-cotton fabric. Here a dozen 1940s Queen Anne–style dining chairs are painted bright red and arranged around an early-eighteenth-century English table. The living room, grounded by a Portuguese needlepoint rug, is a sea of yellow and white that leads the eye to the group portrait that inspired the entire fantastical journey, and which is proudly positioned over the fireplace.

Right In the dramatic entry, a custom-designed dragon-motif rug and coordinating runner introduce the Asian decorative schemes that run throughout the house. Bold colors, such as the red leather on the tufted wing chairs, are played off dark wood floors and white walls to punctuate the space and create memorable moments.

Above In the living room, a chesterfield sofa and a collection of pottery contribute to the sunny-yellow color scheme while accent fabrics incorporate yellow-on-white motifs and enliven the space with a play of pattern on pattern.

Above The painting over the mantel was the inspiration for the color scheme of the entire house; the rug was custom designed and made in Portugal to reflect its use of imperial yellow.

Above Soft curves are present on all the living room furnishings. An antique chair purchased in London is paired with a deeply tufted chesterfield sofa; the curvilinear form of the coffee table adds a subtly sinuous layer to the space.

Opposite Nautical notes dominate the octagonal library. A custom eight-sided rug and gray flannel window shades keep the mood cozy, while a whimsical pattern was chosen for the club chairs to keep the room from taking itself too seriously. The chandelier was found in Paris.

Above and opposite A pair of customized Chinese figures welcomes visitors to the dining room, where Chinese-print fabric covers the walls as well as the windows. A nineteenth-century English table is paired with Queen Anne–style chairs, which were painted a deep Chinese red to create a strong contrast with the room's dominant blue.

Above The kitchen's brass hardware and accessories, such as hanging pendant lamps and an antique scale, speak to the home's seaside location.

Right A large octagonal table commands the breakfast room and begins a bamboo theme that extends to the dining chairs and even to the ceiling above, which is lined with actual canes for texture and exotic appeal.

Left In one of the house's guest rooms, red and yellow create a welcoming and cheerful mood. A striped custom rug coordinates with striped café curtains and a quilted bedspread for a well-appointed but refreshingly simple look.

Above Asian themes creep into this powder room as well. Bamboo detailing appears on the sink's apron, the mirror, and even the wallpaper. A small ceramic dragon completes the motif.

Opposite The bright yellow-and-white color scheme of the living room extends into the master bath. Here brass fittings and a daybed with a classical shape bring a sense of the historic to the space. Matching sinks sit below windows dressed with airy café curtains that allow plenty of ocean light to fill the space.

Above A vintage four-poster bed commands the master bedroom, which continues to draw on the blue and yellow of the living room's painting. A custom rug features a border that ties the whole together.

Opposite and above Each of the guest bedrooms was designed to retain its own character while furthering the decorative schemes introduced in the home's public spaces. A blue-and-white toile cocoon leads to a guest bath fitted with an imperial yellow antique sink and a ceiling genially covered with a surprise oriental-pattern paper.